HAWAI'I'S
HIDDEN PARADISE

GRAHAM OSBORNE

ISLAND HERITAGE™
PUBLISHING

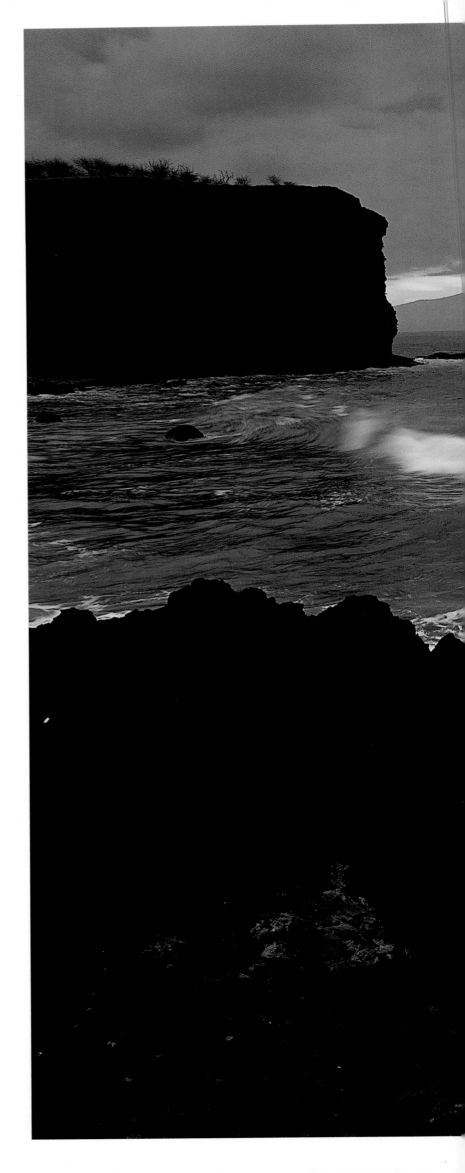

For my little ones, Michael, Maria and little baby.
This book has been done for you with God's help.

Love, Daddy

Dawn breaks over
Pu'u Pehe, Lāna'i

COVER
'Akaka Falls shrouded
in mist, Big Island
of Hawai'i

PREVIOUS PAGE
Last light falls on the
Nāpali Coast, Kaua'i

ISLAND HERITAGE™ PUBLISHING

A DIVISION OF THE MADDEN CORPORATION

94-411 KŌ'AKI STREET, WAIPAHU, HAWAI'I 96797-2806
Orders: (800) 468-2800 • Information: (808) 564-8800
Fax: (808) 564-8877
www.islandheritage.com

ISBN: 1-59700-579-7
First Edition, Second Printing, 2012

Photography copyright ©2008 Graham Osborne

Evening lava flows pour
into the Pacific,
Big Island of Hawai'i

THE AIR WAS WARM AND HUMID, thick with the smell of sulfur and scorched rock. Before me, the earth smoldered and hissed as a relentless train of breakers pounded the newly formed cliffs below. Great clouds of steam and volcanic gas billowed and churned high into the air as a constant stream of lava poured oceanward. It felt as if I had reached the edge of the world.

As dusk approached, things took on an unearthly feel. The massive gas cloud, now towering thousands of feet into the evening sky, pulsed and throbbed in deep magentas and brilliant oranges. Steam pockets exploded, sending showers of molten rock fountaining sixty feet into the air, as lava bomb tracers lit up the night. Occasionally, huge lava bubbles would bulge skyward and suddenly pop in spectacular fashion, sending giant wobbling rings of lava shimmering into the night sky.

I worked feverishly to compose images in the changing light. Sweat poured off my forehead and into the viewfinder, making it difficult to see. My position was good, but I could see that the best views lay about one hundred yards to the north, directly across the system of tubes that carried the magma to the ocean. I eyed the route warily, not thrilled by the prospect of crossing over the smoking rocks, but as the lava display intensified, I decided to scout things out.

As I started tentatively across the subterranean lava tubes, the heat of the magma several feet below me was so intense in places that it threatened to melt my hiking boots. Looking around in the darkness to get my bearings, it was unnerving to discover that I was now encircled by a patchwork of glowing, orange fissures and potholes. In spots, I could actually peer down into magma "skylights" and see the lava flowing a few feet below.

When I finally reached the vantage point I had picked out, I realized to my dismay that the lava fountain had grown quiet. Feeling uneasy in the dark, surrounded by bright orange hot spots and gas vents, I was anxious to cross back over the lava field, but still I decided to wait.

Edging a little closer, I set up my camera, framing my scene based roughly on where I thought all the action had been. To my left, I noticed an intense, orange glow. Peering cautiously over a steep rift in the rocks, I was shocked to discover a huge lava lake over thirty feet across right beside me. It slowly churned and swirled in a great, circular whirlpool, almost hypnotic in its rhythm. I decided it was time to go.

Suddenly, the lava fountain raged to life, hissing and roaring like some great, fiery dragon. The sound was indescribable—like nothing I had heard before. "Too close!" I yelled to myself, as molten lava rocketed high overhead. Abandoning twenty thousand dollar of camera gear and tripod, I scrambled back to high ground to assess the situation. My camera seemed a reasonable distance from the lava spatter zone, but it was still all I could do to muster the courage to go back and retrieve it. Once I got there, however, it was almost impossible not to at least grab a few shots before leaving. It seemed hard to imagine that the walk over the lava field had all been for nothing, so I nervously fired off a series of long exposures, then hastily packed my gear and started the harrowing retreat back across the lava tubes.

Once safely on the other side, I began reflecting back on the wild events of the night, replaying the remarkable images over and over in my mind during the long trail-less hike back in the pitch dark. It had been an extraordinary night of photography, but an equally memorable experience—unlike anything I had ever encountered in my life. I was taken aback by the spectacular beauty and drama that unfolded in a setting like no place else on Earth. This truly is the natural draw of the Hawaiian Islands. Though similar in their geologic history, each island has its own special places and bears a fingerprint that is absolutely unique—diversely stunning in its own right and marvelously different from the surrounding isles. Between the six largest islands in the chain are some of the most exquisite ecosystems in the world, set against some of the most breathtakingly beautiful landscapes on the planet. A lifetime of trekking could not possibly exhaust the countless hidden valleys and rugged coastlines that lie waiting to be explored. While millions live here or have come to visit, there still remains an air of untouched wilderness and primeval mystery to these islands.

The "Big Island" of Hawai'i is the perfect example of this. The largest and most southern of all the islands, it is a remarkable place. Center stage is Hawai'i Volcanoes National Park. To hike out across the contorted, volcanic flood plains and watch as molten lava pours endlessly into the steaming froth of the Pacific is like watching a chapter from the Creation account of Genesis unfold before your eyes, the earth literally being formed and molded as you watch.

Equally stunning can be walking the floor of Kīlauea Crater at dawn, surrounded by swirling mist glowing honey-yellow in the early rays of sunrise. Literally thousands of fissures and vents release steam and volcanic gases into the still, morning air here, transforming the landscape into mysterious patterns of changing shapes and forms.

Carrying on into the surrounding *hāpu'u* tree fern forests that have colonized the older lava flows, the most perfect symphony of Nature imaginable awaits the early morning and evening hiker. Countless tropical songbirds chorus unseen from the forest canopy, their elegant, high harmonies blending to perfection.

Running eastward from here is the Puna coastline. Far from the rushing crowds, the natural rhythm of the sea rules here. Paralleled by a narrow one lane road, it is like stepping back into old Hawai'i. Intimate palm-trimmed, lava rock bays alternate with spectacular groves of tropical rainforest. Venturing inland, great stands of lava trees form delicate tapestries far above the forest floor, exceeding even the most intricate of lacework patterns. Come evening, the chorus of frogs and songbirds that echoes through the forest can be hauntingly mesmerizing.

Moving further north, the Hāmākua Coast is indented by countless small rainforest valleys that drain the slopes above. Several little paved tracks spur off the main road and wind along charming little rainforest creeks, many of which are paralleled by narrow game trails that lead past exquisite, fern-edged grottos and tumbling punchbowl falls. Here, one can truly experience the essence of the rainforest. Tarzan-like vines and greenery vie for space along side these lush water courses, and jewel-like pools lay hidden deep in the jungle for those willing to look.

Heading inland toward the heart of the island, a great "saddle" cuts between the two massive shield volcanoes that dominate the Big Island—Mauna Loa and Mauna Kea. Unique in their own right, the lofty peaks of these two mammoths are both capable of sporting snow, especially in the winter months. At lower elevations, scuttling low clouds and fog are common elements, regularly shrouding the landscape of cinder cones, lava plains, and *koa* forests in a veil of eerie mist. A land of raw, stark beauty, the conditions that have formed this almost alien valley exist nowhere else in the world.

To the west of the saddle lies a surprising band of volcanic grassland that rivals the great prairies of central North America for their beauty. Rolling hills and plains stretch for miles, delicately trimmed in a soft peach fuzz of showy bunch grasses, their conspicuous seed heads glowing luminously in the soft backlight of morning and evening. This is a place of patterns and rhythms, delighting the eye with its simple order.

To the northern tip of the island, the great Kohala cliffs rise majestically out of the Pacific. There is perhaps no better place on the islands to take in the sunrise here. The right morning can yield absolutely astounding views to the east, as rich, honeyed light bathes the steaming cliffs in golden mist.

From here, one can often see the island of Maui lying to the north, the dominant dome of Haleakalā Volcano soaring high above the fringe of puffy cumulous clouds that often encircles it. Skirting Haleakalā's northern base is the Hāna Coast. The almost incessant upslope cloud and precipitation that forms here results in a lush, Garden of Eden-like setting. Many come to visit this famous coastline, but often turn back at the town of Hāna, long before the hairpin

Tropical rainforest in the
mist, Nanue Valley,
Big Island of Hawai'i

road takes on a more laid-back, intimate feel. Some of the best waterfalls on the islands can be found here, many with their own distinctive character, but the sheer number of cascades alone is impressive.

To the opposite end of the island lies the West Maui Mountains. Often overlooked, the steep-sided valleys that carve their way into the western heart of this range remain largely unexplored and spectacular. The eastern flanks of these same mountains are equally striking. A narrow one-lane road winds tentatively along this ragged coast, revealing one of the most desolately beautiful shorelines on the islands. Lunar-like rock formations are highlighted by spectacular blow holes, deep amethyst-green tidal pools, and wild crashing surf. All of this is far from the bustle that can be found on other parts of the island.

Not to be outdone, O'ahu stands as the most visited of all the islands. Without question, it has taken the brunt of the pressure from the encroaching civilization, but at its core, it remains absolutely spectacular. Few views in the world can challenge first light on the eastern face of the Ko'olau Range. Heavy rains have etched deep erosion columns into the sheer face of these mountains, as they rise cathedral-like from the valley floor. Draped in lush green vegetation, they evoke visions of a primordial landscape, wildly pristine and untamed. To my mind, they are some of the most awe-inspiring spires in the world.

In contrast, their arid cousins that lie along the less populated western spine of the island are almost their equal in grandeur. Far less visited, their craggy, often barren, rock walls present a more intimidating presence. Late evening light can reveal rugged textures and shapes, making a dramatic backdrop to a coastline that alternates between long sandy beaches, rocky outcrops, and reefs—a photographer's dream.

The North Shore is well known for the monster waves it generates during the winter storm season, but the southeast tip of O'ahu also boasts some extreme surf, and is by far the more impressive, visually. Looming ominously on the skyline here is the extinct Koko Head Crater. Perfectly cone shaped, its sides are deeply but symmetrically etched with erosion gullies, giving it a very imposing footprint. The shoreline itself is a mix of sculpted, rocky headlands and layered cliffs, honeycombed with great caverns and surge channels. When the wind and seas are right, absolute chaos ensues. Huge waves violently pummel the rock walls without relief, exploding with extraordinary fury and sending tumultuous eruptions of spray and foam rocketing skyward. Arguably, this is one of the better places on the islands to watch big wave action.

Switching gears a bit, Moloka'i is the perfect chaser to the busier pace of O'ahu. World-renowned for the massive sea cliffs that grace much of Moloka'i's northern coast, the cliffs themselves are difficult to view well unless you go by boat, plane, or donkey! I still recall days of searching trail after trail, trying to bushwhack my way to a good overlook of these cliffs. On one particular morning, I had just about given up hope when I discovered a little dirt track near Ho'olehua that headed straight north. As I crested a little knoll at the end of the road, suddenly, there lay the cliffs in all their panoramic glory. Ochre mist drifted across them

Yokohama Bay and surf
in evening light, O'ahu

emphasizing the repeating layers and valleys that receded to the east as far as the eye could see. The misty cliffs positively glowed in the early morning backlight, and it remains one of the most memorable scenes from all my travels on the islands.

Along Moloka'i's backbone of inland peaks lies the great Kamakou Preserve. Securing some of the finest tracts of native Hawaiian rainforest left in the world, thick jungle alternates between steep forested hillsides and boggy swamps. The diversity of life here is bewildering, and at times, the forest can be almost visually overwhelming.

Further to the south, the much drier Mo'omomi Preserve features rolling sand dunes and wave-chiseled, rocky bays that stretch for miles. Shaped by pounding surf and almost constant northeast trade winds, this unique preserve protects more rare coastal species than any other place in the main Hawaiian Islands and serves as a critical nesting ground for the endangered green sea turtle. With a rugged, windswept beauty, it is a step back in time to an ecosystem that once thrived across the islands, but is now sadly reduced to a few meager remnants.

Directly across the channel to the south of Moloka'i lies the island of Lāna'i. Perhaps the most laid-back of all the Hawaiian Islands, very few paved roads traverse it, leaving Lāna'i best viewed by four wheel drive, boat, or mountain bike. Pu'u Pehe (Sweetheart Rock) is one exception. Being easily reached by road, it is a grand place to watch the sun rise brilliant and orange over Shark Bay and the distant mountains of Maui.

But to my mind, Lāna'i's crown jewel lies along its western coastline. Jutting sharply out of the Pacific, the great *palis* (cliffs) that edge this side of the island are second only to

Moloka'i's in size. Stretching for miles, they are dotted with grottos, sea caves, and secluded coves. Midway along this shore stands the striking Nānāhoa (Three Stones,) a collections of sea stacks that rise majestically from the Pacific, like great sentinels keeping watch over Lāna'i's western flank.

To the interior, some of Hawai'i's finest "red dirt" terrain can be found. Benches and rolling hills are interspersed with deeply eroded gulches sporting rainbow arrays of reds, oranges, and yellows. Dotted with peculiar collections of rounded rocks and outcroppings, there is a surreal, fantasy feel to this landscape, and the reds and oranges of the soil can appear almost unnatural in their intensity.

To the south, secluded, golden beaches stretch out endlessly, with panoramic views of nearby Moloka'i to the north at every turn. There are places on this little island where you could go all day and not see another soul, and it can be a refreshing change from the frantic pace of the rest of the world.

At the northern end of this great volcanic chain lies Kaua'i. Often referred to as the "Garden Isle," it does not disappoint.

At the visual heart of the island stand the mountains of the Nāpali Coast. Unlike any mountain range on Earth, they defy description: razor-edged ridge lines and pinnacles, plummeting vertical walls, and narrowly spaced erosion channels pleating the heavily vegetated spires of volcanic rock. There is no place equal to the Nāpali Coast .

The view of this coastline from Kē'ē Beach is exceptional, and may be one of the finest places to watch the sun set anywhere in the world. Rosy clouds usually drape the ridge tops as the mist from the transpiring cliffs glows brilliant orange and yellow, accentuating the repeating ridges and folds that tightly line the rock faces. There is something almost prehistoric about this coast and it is unmatched in its unique beauty. Virtually untracked and impenetrable, it remains a pristine wilderness holdout against the onslaught of development that has besieged other parts of the islands—a truly international treasure.

Backdropping the Nāpali Range is Waimea Canyon. Hawai'i's own version of the Grand Canyon, it is a dizzying drop to the valley floor from the many viewpoints along the canyon's western perimeter. The iridescent reds and oranges that paint the canyon walls look almost unreal in just about any light, but the beautiful low light of morning accentuates the rugged textures and rock outcrops better than at any other time of day. Some of the best views in all the islands are to be found here, with options to hike out along ridges to the great canyon headwalls, work northwest and plunge deep into the heart of the Nāpali cliffs, or to turn northeast and disappear into the lush rainforests and perched bogs of the almost mystical realm of Alaka'i Swamp and Mount Wai'ale'ale, the wettest spot on Earth. All this and much more makes Kaua'i one of my absolute favorite islands to photograph.

With such diversity and unparalleled scenery, it is not hard to see why the world is drawn to these diamonds of the Pacific. The Hawaiian Islands are truly a land of superlatives without equal, the quintessential tropical paradise.

But within their great attraction also lies the seed to their demise. Despite sustaining enormous pressure from within and without, the Hawaiian Islands have still maintained much of their natural wilderness. There are still many places on the islands where one can feel they are the last person on Earth. But great care and foresight must be exercised here, by Hawaiians and visitors alike. Here lies a natural heritage that is for all peoples of the world, both present and future, and we will have lost much if one day we realize that we have left the garden too long untended.

We have been set as stewards over this irreplaceable corner of Creation. Let us not bury our talents and wait for others to do what we have been charged with. It is my hope that these images can contribute to this end—moments of light that have simply captured God's great work here. What a profound privilege it has been.

Graham Osborne

Hāmākua Coast at dusk,
Big Island of Hawaiʻi

FOLLOWING SPREADS
Waterfall and ferns, Hāna
coast, Maui

Sunrise over North Kohala
cliffs, Big Island of Hawaiʻi

Waves wash over a rocky
reef at twilight, Kaluako'i,
Moloka'i

FOLLOWING SPREADS
Volcanic gases glow golden
in first light, Kīlauea Crater
floor, Big Island of Hawai'i

Sea cliffs in morning mist,
northern coast of Moloka'i

Incoming breaker explodes
on lava spires, Laupāhoehoe
Point, Big Island of Hawai'i

FOLLOWING SPREAD
Hālona coast in dawn
alpenglow, O'ahu

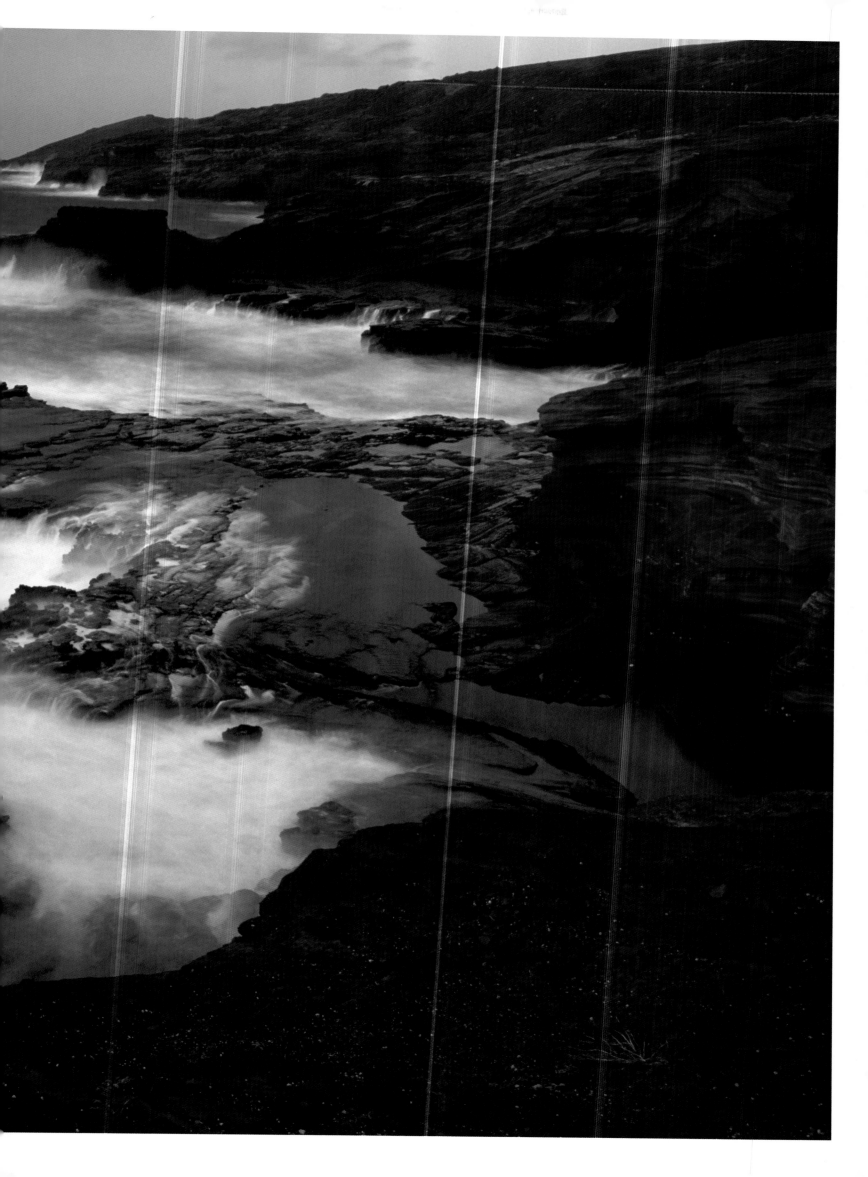

Massive waves explode in the
sea caves along the Hālona
coast, Oʻahu

FACING PAGE
Ragged shoreline along
Poʻelua Bay, Maui

Eucalyptus canopy in mist
on the flanks of Haleakalā
Volcano, Maui

FACING PAGE
Eucalyptus tree details,
Hāna coast, Maui

Koko Crater in afternoon
light, O'ahu

Hills above Mānele Bay, Lāna'i

FACING PAGE

The arid peaks of Mākaha
Valley, O'ahu

South Kohala grasslands,
Parker Ranch,
Big Island of Hawai'i

FACING PAGE
Rolling grasslands and lava
plains with Mauna Loa
behind, Big Island of Hawai'i

Sunrise over Puʻu Pehe and
Shark Bay, Lānaʻi

Palm silhouettes, Place of
Refuge, Big Island of Hawai'i

FACING PAGE
'Āhihi Bay in the magenta
afterglow of sunset, Maui

FOLLOWING SPREAD
Kona sunset,
Big Island of Hawai'i

Limahuli Valley, eastern end of
the Nāpali Coast, Kauaʻi

Waterfalls in flood,
Hāna coast, Maui

FACING PAGE
Palm-fringed bay along the
Puna coast,
Big Island of Hawai'i

Makaweli lithified cliffs,
Poʻipū coast, Kauaʻi

FACING PAGE
Moonlight bathes the
southeast tip of the
Big Island of Hawaiʻi

Hāpuʻu tree fern forest,
Hawaiʻi Volcanoes National
Park, Big Island of Hawaiʻi

FACING PAGE
Koʻolau Range in first light,
Oʻahu

Branch patterns near Kahului,
Maui

FACING PAGE
'Ohe'o Gulch, Haleakalā
National Park, Maui

FOLLOWING SPREAD
Nāpali cliffs veiled in
golden mist, Kaua'i

Sunburst over Kaʻiwa Point,
Poʻipū coast, Kauaʻi

FOLLOWING SPREADS
Sea cave at Nānāhoa, Lānaʻi

Moonrise over Puna coast,
Big Island of Hawaiʻi

A wilderness valley cuts deep
into the heart of the West
Maui Mountains, Maui

FACING PAGE
Red earth formations along
Halulu Gulch, Lānaʻi

Grasslands near Puʻuanahulu,
Big Island of Hawaiʻi

FACING PAGE
Fallen *kiawe* tree and cinder
cone, Kohala Mountains,
Big Island of Hawaiʻi

Rainbow Falls,
Big Island of Hawai'i

Kapehu Stream near
Hilo Bay, Hāmākua Coast,
Big Island of Hawai'i

FACING PAGE
Wailua Falls,
Hāna coast, Maui

FOLLOWING SPREAD
Tide pool at sunset, Hōnaunau
Bay, Big Island of Hawai'i

Lava patterns and palms,
Place of Refuge,
Big Island of Hawai'i

FACING PAGE
Pu'uhonua Point at last light,
Big Island of Hawai'i

West Maui Mountains in
evening light, Maui

Waimea Canyon in morning
light, Kauaʻi

FACING PAGE
Moʻomomi dunes at dawn,
Molokaʻi

Koko Head coastline
at sunrise, O'ahu

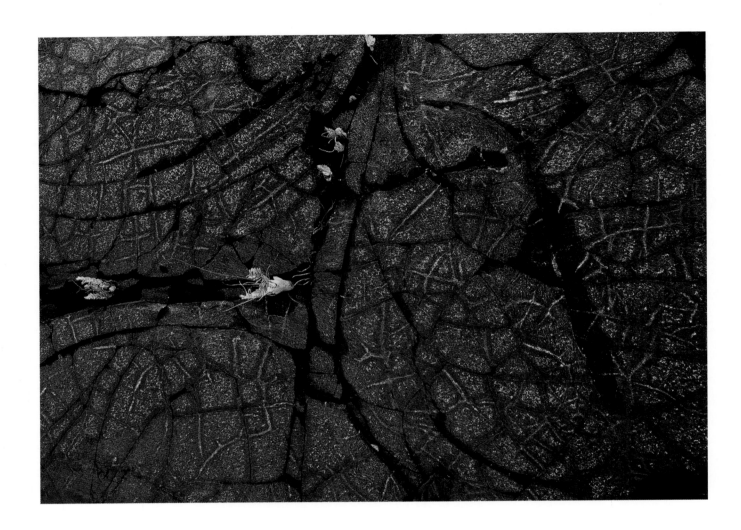

Lava patterns, Puʻuloa,
Hawaiʻi Volcanoes National
Park, Big Island of Hawaiʻi

FACING PAGE
Submarine Rock, Hālona
coast, Oʻahu

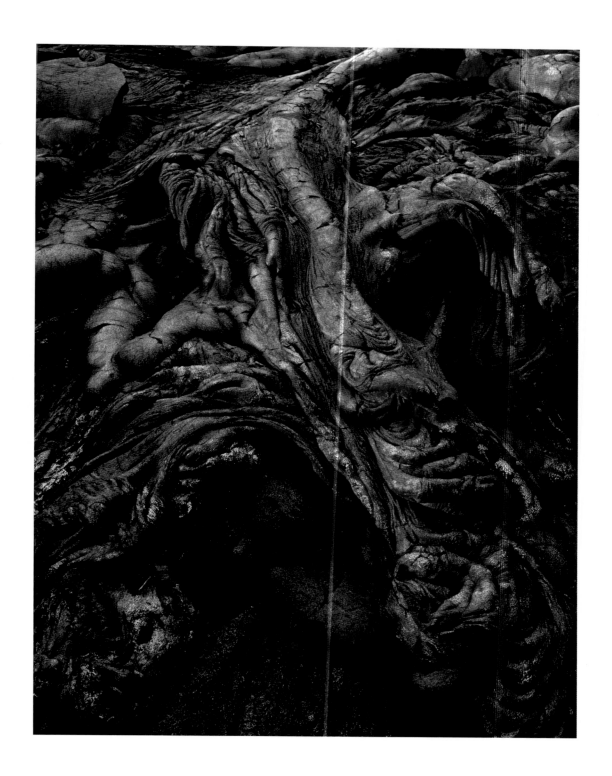

Ancient *pāhoehoe* (smooth lava)
flow glows orange in reflected
evening light, Hōlei Pali,
Big Island of Hawai'i

FACING PAGE
Lava fountain, Hawai'i Volcanoes
National Park,
Big Island of Hawai'i

Pāhoehoe (smooth lava)
patterns, Kīlauea Volcano,
Big Island of Hawai'i

FACING PAGE
South Kona coast at sunset,
Big Island of Hawai'i

Waves thunder in
early morning light,
Laupāhoehoe Point,
Big Island of Hawai'i

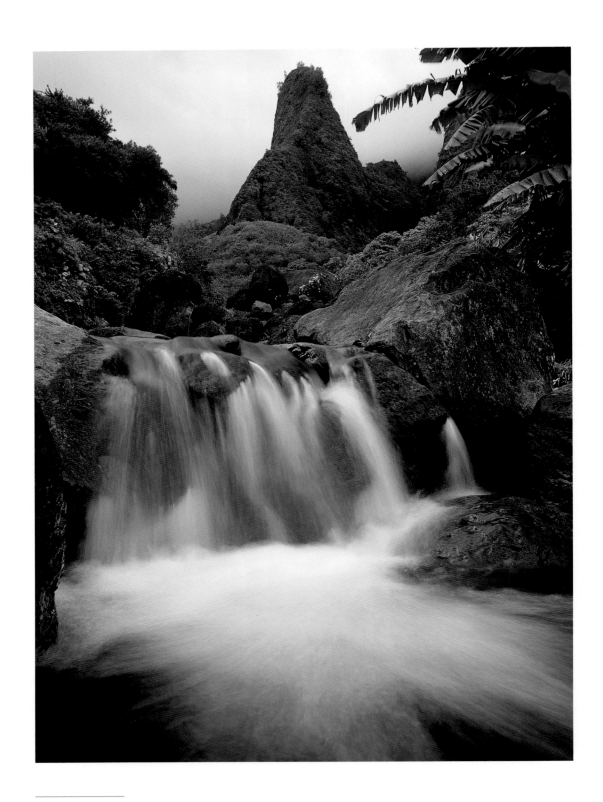

'Īao Needle, Maui

FACING PAGE
Kaholo Pali and Shark Fin Rock at
Kaunolū, west coast of Lāna'i

FOLLOWING SPREAD
Koko Head coastline at dusk, O'ahu

Last light on
Kahakuloa Head,
Mōkōlea Point, Maui

FACING PAGE
Rainbow over Moloka'i,
Kapalua coast, Maui

Volcanic steam cloud rises over cliffs and massive breakers, Puna coast, Big Island of Hawai'i

Surf washes over coral
reef terraces at sunset,
Kēʻē Beach, Kauaʻi

FACING PAGE
Exposed reef and surf,
Kona coast,
Big Island of Hawaiʻi

Rugged coastline of
Yokohama Bay, Oʻahu

Koʻolau Range reflections at
first light, Oʻahu

Lava tree canopy silhouettes,
Kapoho, Big Island of Hawai'i

Nāpali Coast mountains
in evening light, Kaua'i

FACING PAGE
Kalalau Valley,
Kōke'e State Park, Kaua'i

Kiawe tree patterns,
Moloka'i

FACING PAGE
Honolua Stream and
forest, Maui

Salt marsh, south coast
of Moloka'i

Wailua falls in rosy mist
of dawn, Kaua'i

FACING PAGE
Storm over Kamakou
Preserve rainforest, Moloka'i

FOLLOWING SPREADS
Moonrise over Olivine Pools,
north coast of Maui

Reef surge channel,
Shark's Cove, North Shore
of O'ahu

FOLLOWING SPREAD
Sun pierces morning clouds
over the Hāmākua Coast,
Big Island of Hawai'i

Evening light shafts through
cumulous clouds over Maui

FACING PAGE
Golden waves surge into
Kawaʻaloa Bay at sunrise,
Molokaʻi

Egrets at sunrise,

North Kohala cliffs,

Big Island of Hawai'i